887

Selected works by Robert Lepage
(in translation)

The Seven Streams of the River Ota
Polygraph (with Marie Brassard)
Elsinore
The Blue Dragon (with Marie Michaud)

887

A PLAY

ROBERT LEPAGE

Including "Speak White"
by Michèle Lalonde

Preface
by Denys Arcand

Translated by
Louisa Blair

ARACHNIDE

Original text from the theatre play *887* copyright © 2015 Robert Lepage
Copyright © 2016 L'instant même (Text edition)
Copyright © 2016 Éditions Québec Amérique, Inc. (Illustrated edition)
English translation copyright © 2018 Louisa Blair
"Speak White," poem, copyright © 1968 Michèle Lalonde

Published in Canada in 2019 and the USA in 2019 by House of Anansi Press Inc.
www.houseofanansi.com

House of Anansi Press is committed to protecting our natural environment.
As part of our efforts, the interior of this book is printed on paper that contains 100%
post-consumer recycled fibres, is acid-free, and is processed chlorine-free.

23 22 21 20 19   1 2 3 4 5

Library and Archives Canada Cataloguing in Publication

Title: 887 / Robert Lepage ; preface by Denys Arcand ; translated by Louisa Blair.
Other titles: 887. English | Eight hundred eighty-seven
Names: Lepage, Robert, 1957– author. | Arcand, Denys, 1941 June 25– writer of preface.
| Blair, Louisa, translator. | Lalonde, Michèle, 1937– Speak white.
Description: Translation of: 887. | A play. | "Including "Speak white"
by Michèle Lalonde" — Title page.
Identifiers: Canadiana (print) 20189002298 | Canadiana (ebook) 20189002301 | ISBN
9781487003920 (softcover) | ISBN 9781487003937 (EPUB) | ISBN 9781487003944 (Kindle)
Classification: LCC PS8573.E635 A61813 2018 | DDC C842/.54—dc23

Library of Congress Control Number: 2018931769

Originator of translation project: Lynda Beaulieu
Publication project manager (Ex Machina): Édouard Garneau
Publication project collaborator: Marie-Pierre Gagné
Stage directions, editing, and translation review: Normand Bissonnette
Copyeditor: Gemma Wain
Proofreader: Elizabeth Mitchell

Cover design: Adapted from the original by Anne-Marie Jacques
Cover photograph: Erick Labbé
Text design and typesetting: Sara Loos and Laura Brady

Canada Council | Conseil des Arts
for the Arts | du Canada

ONTARIO ARTS COUNCIL
CONSEIL DES ARTS DE L'ONTARIO
an Ontario government agency
un organisme du gouvernement de l'Ontario

*We acknowledge for their financial support of our publishing program the Canada Council
for the Arts, the Ontario Arts Council, and the Government of Canada.*

Printed and bound in Canada

In memory of my father

PREFACE

Robert Lepage is at his most eloquent when he talks about himself. Luckily, he often does. Sometimes it's from behind a mask — of history, culture, travel or language — but other times, he's simply himself, baring his whole heart and soul. That's how I like him best.

Most authors who talk about themselves are trying to either glorify, justify or excuse themselves. Writers like Montaigne or Pepys, who tell us who they really are without disguise, are rare. Yet these revelations are what we prize most because they give us some respite from our fundamental solitude: we recognize ourselves in them. When Robert speaks to us of his childhood, his adolescence, his loves, we are sharing the human condition with him. And this sharing is the primary mission of art.

In theatre, playwrights tend to wear the masks of their characters. In the character of Alceste, we can sense Molière's own painful love for a flirtatious coquette. But Alceste is not altogether Molière. His traits are slightly exaggerated so they express the wisdom of Philinte too, who is also Molière. Great dramatists are all their characters at once.

In *887*, we get the feeling there is no disconnect between Robert and his character. We are with him in his kitchen, with poor old Fred from Radio-Canada. We are with him when he steps onstage at the beginning to ask us, somewhat disingenuously, to turn off our phones — a cunning sleight of hand that announces the magic of the whole show. The magic works on us all the more because Robert is a man against whom we are powerless. His brilliant simplicity is irresistible.

I fell under his spell a long time ago, backstage in a suburban theatre after the show *Vinci*. I succumbed after just a few words. We later made two films together, and each day I couldn't wait to meet up with him on the set, to chat, to laugh, to bitch about annoying people, and to rejoice in everything we loved. I have cultured friends — people who've read every book, or seen every work of art, or played every piece of music. But Robert's culture is absolutely unique, and I still can't quite put my finger on it. The main element is probably his insatiable curiosity about every culture in the world. Every time I run across that area of London with the unlikely name of Elephant and Castle, I remember it was Robert who told me that its name was a corruption of *Infanta de Castille*. That's the kind of thing he knows. Just like he knows that "speak white" originally came from the American cotton plantations.

But in Robert, this global culture coexists with deep roots in Quebec culture. When I saw *The Dragons' Trilogy* (in Paris, *figurez-vous!*), I was blown away at how the life story of the Chinese launderer revealed such deep historical roots. I can't remember who said that the universal is the local without walls, but it applies perfectly to *887*. As he narrates his childhood and adolescent memories, which seem so simple, he is actually retelling Quebec history from 1960 to 1970: the designing of the Canadian flag, General de Gaulle's visit, Pierre Bourgault, and even the shifting social origins of the students at the Conservatoire d'art dramatique de Québec. Indeed, there is a particularly acute awareness of class in *887*, from the despicable way Robert was refused admission to a private school to his profound understanding of Michèle Lalonde's poem.

Robert probably isn't given enough credit for his writing, or for his sense of humour. The expression *fêlé du bolo* ("cracked in the head") brought back my entire childhood in an instant. And I love the sonority of the name "Nancy Nolet", the poor Brit who serves high tea at the Château Frontenac, and the image of Johnny Farago being born in an amphitheatre full of medical students at Université Laval.

In general, fathers don't come off very well in Quebec literature and drama. They are often the scapegoats for our writers — and especially for women writers. They are absent, weak-willed or cowardly, when they're not drunk or violent. In these figures I never recognize my own father, grandfather or uncles, who were strong, calm and respectful men. *887* is a love letter from Robert to his father. It touches me very deeply. His father spent time in the navy; mine stayed all his life. Like Robert's father, mine was a man of few words. He died thirty years ago, and I still miss him. Which is why I came away from *887* feeling so moved and so happy.

DENYS ARCAND

887 pre-premiered in its original French version at the lieu unique theatre, in Nantes, on February 24, 2015. The world premiere of the show (in English, translation by Louisa Blair) was at the Bluma Appel Theatre on July 14, 2015, as part of Panamania, the Arts and Culture Program of the 2015 Pan Am and Parapan Am Games in Toronto.

Special thanks to the artists and artisans who have contributed to the success of *887.*

Written, designed, directed, and performed by Robert Lepage

Creative direction and design	Steve Blanchet
Dramaturg	Peder Bjurman
Assistant director	Adèle Saint-Amand
Composer and sound designer	Jean-Sébastien Côté
Lighting designer	Laurent Routhier
Image designer	Félix Fradet-Faguy
Associate set designer	Sylvain Décarie
Associate properties designer	Ariane Sauvé
Associate costume designer	Jeanne Lapierre
Production manager	Marie-Pierre Gagné
Production assistant	Véronique St-Jacques

Technical director	Paul Bourque
Tour manager	Samuel Sauvageau
Technical director (touring)	Olivier Bourque
Stage manager	Nadia Bélanger
Sound manager	Olivier Marcil
Lighting manager	Elliot Gaudreau
Multimedia integration and video manager	Nicolas Dostie
Costume and properties manager	Isabel Poulin
Head stagehand	Chloé Blanchet
Technical consultants	Catherine Guay
	Tobie Horswill
Acting consultant (creative process)	Reda Guerinik
Director's agent	Lynda Beaulieu

Additional poem: "Speak White," poem © 1968 by Michèle Lalonde, used with permission of Michèle Lalonde.

Michèle Lalonde's bilingual poem takes the form of a dramatic riposte to the famous command "Speak white!" once used on the North American plantations to order slaves to speak in the language of their white masters. Later the expression was used to urge French-speaking Canadians to speak English and to remind them of their inferiority or subordinate position.

Additional music:

"Mer Morte," by Jean-Guy Cossette and Gilles Morissette. Éditions Densta and Macadam Cow-Girl. Performed by Arthur et les Jaguars. Used by permission of Disques Mérite.

"Bang Bang (My Baby Shot Me Down)," by Sonny Bono. © Cotillion Music Inc. and Chris-Marc Music. Performed by

Nancy Sinatra. Used by permission of Boots Enterprises, Inc.

"Bang Bang (My Baby Shot Me Down)," by Sonny Bono. © Cotillion Music Inc. and Chris-Marc Music. French adaptation performed by Claire Lepage. Used by permission of Disques Mérite.

"Mood Indigo," by Edward Kennedy Ellington, Irving Mills, and Albany Bigard. Performed by Henry Mancini and his Orchestra © 1960. Used by permission of Sony/ATV Music Publishing and the Songwriters Guild of America for Indigo Mood Music.

"Leavin' On Your Mind," by Michael Webb Pierce and Wayne P. Walker. Universal Songs of Polygram International, Inc. Performed by Patsy Cline. Used by permission of Universal Music Publishing Canada.

Nocturne in C Minor, Op. 48, No. 1, by Frédéric Chopin. Performed by Martin Gauthier.

Minuet No. 2, by Johann Sebastian Bach. Arrangement by Gabriel Thibaudeau. Performed by Gabriel Thibaudeau and Denis Chabot.

Additional images:

Photo of Donald Gordon. CSTM/Collection CN: X-40842. Used by permission of the Canada Science and Technology Museum.

A View of the Taking of Quebec September 13th 1759 (1797), Hervey Smythe. Public domain.

James Murray (c. 1765–1770), unknown artist. Public domain.

Portrait of Major-General James Wolfe (1727–1759) as a Young Man (1749), attributed to Joseph Highmore. Public domain.

An Ex Machina production commissioned by the Arts and
Culture Program of the Toronto 2015 Pan Am and Parapan
Am Games.
    In coproduction with:

    Le lieu unique, Nantes
    La Comète — Scène nationale de Châlons-en-
        Champagne
    Edinburgh International Festival
    Aarhus Festuge
    Théâtre de la Ville — Paris
    Festival d'Automne à Paris
    Romaeuropa Festival 2015
    Bonlieu — Scène nationale, Annecy
    Ysarca Art Promotions — Pilar de Yzaguirre
    Célestins — Théâtre de Lyon
    SFU's 50th Anniversary Cultural Program, Simon
        Fraser University, Vancouver
    National Arts Centre French Theatre, Ottawa
    Théâtre du Nouveau Monde, Montreal
    Tokyo Metropolitan Theatre
    Théâtre du Trident, Quebec

La Coursive — Scène nationale, La Rochelle
Canadian Stage, Toronto

Producer for Ex Machina: Michel Bernatchez (assisted by Vanessa Landry-Claverie and Valérie Lambert)

Associate producer, Europe and Japan: Epidemic (Richard Castelli, assisted by Chara Skiadelli, Florence Berthaud, and Claire Dugot)

Associate producer, Americas, Asia (except Japan), Australia and New Zealand: Menno Plukker Theatre Agent (Menno Plukker, assisted by Dominique Sarrazin and Isaïe Richard).

PROLOGUE

The house lights are still up when Robert Lepage, in a black suit and white shirt, enters stage right. The lights go down imperceptibly during the prologue. He stands downstage. Behind him is a large black rectangle of two sliding partitions flanked by black legs. The only thing on the stage is a prompter's box at his feet.

He addresses the audience.

Good evening everyone, and welcome to (*name of performance venue*) for this performance of *887*, a new creation by Ex Machina.

Before we begin, I've been asked to remind you of the house rules. So if you would take a moment to turn off your cellphones, your pagers or any other electronic gadgets that could disturb the performance. We'd like to remind you that the show will last for two hours with no intermission. In case of emergency please use one of the (*number of exits in venue*) emergency exits.

The show will begin in just a few moments, but first I'd like to take a minute to talk to you about the origins of this theatre project about memory. The idea came to me a few years ago, in 2010, when I was invited to take part in the 40th anniversary of that famous poetry night at the Monument-National in Montreal.

The evening was a tribute to the famous "Nuit de la poésie" in the spring of 1970, which to this day is considered the foundational event of contemporary Québécois poetry.

For the occasion, they asked all sorts of famous people to come and reread the same poems as forty years ago, and in more or less the same order. I was deeply honoured that they asked me to read Michèle Lalonde's poem "Speak White," hardly a negligible poem, and which in fact probably had more influence on Quebec's social and political consciousness in the 1960s and '70s than any other.

And since there were going to be all kinds of people up on stage for whom reciting poetry was not their strongest suit, they asked me if I could possibly learn my poem by heart. It would make the evening a little less formal and also there would be less shifting around of lecterns and mic stands.

I agreed right away, thinking that learning it would be a piece of cake as the poem is only three pages long and I had a full week ahead of me to memorize it. So I settled down at my place one Sunday morning with a cup of coffee, and after several hours of trying, I was still absolutely incapable of remembering a single line.

I wondered if it was the slightly peculiar form of the poem that made it so difficult to memorize, or if it was just that once you hit fifty, you not only become a little hard of hearing but also, as we say in Quebec, *fêlé du bolo*, or one doughnut short of a dozen.

Still, I comforted myself with the thought that it was probably a bit of fatigue and a lot of intellectual laziness, because like most of you here tonight, I've come to rely too much on these little gadgets (*shows his smartphone*) to remember stuff for me. Practically my whole life is in this thing: my schedule for the next four or five years, all my contacts, my addresses, my phone numbers. I don't even have to know my own phone number anymore. I just touch a little icon and it magically pops up on the screen. Seriously, if you asked me for my private number right now I wouldn't have a clue.

Yet I have no trouble remembering my very first phone number from when I was a kid.

The sliding partitions open like curtains to reveal a projection screen with the number "681-5031" projected on it.

It was 681-5031.

For some obscure reason this sequence of numbers, which is totally useless to me and probably no longer in service, is permanently etched into my frontal lobe. This suggests one thing at least: that long-term memory seems to be more persistent, while short-term memory gets more fragile and disintegrates as we grow older.

To help me memorize this famous poem, I used an old mnemonic trick that apparently dates back to the ancient Greeks. It's called the Memory Palace. What's a Memory Palace? What you do is this: Think of a place you knew well when you were very young. It can be a place where you once lived, or just where you spent a lot of time, like your school, or the rec centre. Then you take the sentences or paragraphs of the text you have to memorize and put them in lots of different spots in the various rooms of your Memory Palace. Then when you need to remember it all, you just go back in your mind to your Memory Palace and gather up the pieces of what you have to recite.

So I thought my Memory Palace would probably be at . . .

He gets his cellphone out of his pocket and uses it like a remote control. He points it at the screen and "887, avenue Murray" appears.

887 Murray Avenue, in Quebec city.

As he speaks, he puts his hand on the right-hand edge of the screen and pushes it, causing it to rotate on an invisible turntable. What appeared to be just a screen is actually the side wall of a huge model of the building where he grew up, like a giant doll's house. It is a minutely faithful reproduction on a scale of 1:6, just over two metres tall. It stops rotating when the front of the building is facing the audience. It is an apartment building with eight apartments, two per floor: two at the semi-basement level, each with a living room window; the other six also with windows but with balconies and balcony doors too. In the centre are the entrance and the stairwell windows. Each window is in fact an LCD screen so the interiors can light up and come to life as the scene requires.

This is the address of the apartment building where I lived with my family from 1960 to 1970. In Quebec, this corresponds more or less to the period between the start of the Quiet Revolution and the end of the October Crisis.

887 — THE APARTMENT BUILDING

As Robert talks about the apartments one by one, the occupants of each are visible through the windows, going about their daily activities.

We lived here, in Apartment 5. It was a three-bedroom apartment. Of course in my child's memory it seemed huge. But in fact it was quite cramped for a family consisting of a father, a mother and four children.

Our upstairs neighbours, in Apartment 7, were the Robsons. Mr. Robson was a Canadian of Irish descent who had married a Québécoise. They had three children: Wayne, Gordon and Gale. Like most Irish Catholics at the time, they were very devout. They went to mass every Sunday. Mrs. Robson suffered from an obsessive-compulsive disorder when it came to cleanliness, and insisted her children go to confession at least once a week to make sure their souls were as spotless as her kitchen counter.

But the Robsons weren't the only English-Canadian family living in the building. There were also the Saint Moores, here in Apartment 4. Mr. Saint Moore had died several years earlier, and the children were all old enough to have moved out on their own. The only one left was Louis Saint Moore — you can see him there with his crutches — who lived alone with his mother. Louis had once been a piano teacher at the music school, where he met a pretty young concert violinist. Unfortunately, on their way to announce their engagement to her parents, as they were driving through an immense national park north of Quebec city, they hit a moose. The car flipped over several times before plunging into a lake. The young woman drowned, and poor Louis Saint Moore was left with shattered legs and a shattered heart.

In Apartment 1, it was the Côté family, whom we had nicknamed the Gorilla Family, because the children were all totally wild. They climbed all over the walls, swung from the curtains . . . People said it was because Mrs. Côté used to work as a cashier at the zoo in Orsainville, and that one day she probably fell into the gorilla's cage, and he grabbed the opportunity to try to save his endangered species.

Apartment 2 was where Mr. Serge Vicière lived. He was a high school French teacher. Mr. Vicière could have easily afforded a better place on his teacher's salary, but he preferred to save up his money to bring the rest of his family over from Haiti.

This is his mother you can see here, hanging up the laundry in the living room. She said it was too cold and humid in Quebec to hang her laundry outside, but the real reason was that they didn't have the money to buy curtains. This was her way of shielding herself from the curiosity of the passers-by, who had clearly never seen a Black family before.

In Apartment 3 was the Gauthier family. Actually, they weren't really a family, they were barely even a couple. He worked as a longshoreman in the port of Quebec and she acted as the concierge of the building. They had no children but they did have a Great Dane called Prince, who barked all the time and terrorized the whole building. When I was small I was so afraid of dogs that I avoided walking by Apartment 3 because I was convinced that Prince would break the door down and eat me for lunch.

Apartment 8 was where Johnny Farago's family lived. Yes, seriously, the famous Johnny Farago, before he moved to Montreal and became a big Québécois popstar. Here he is, at age twelve, doing one of his famous Elvis Presley impersonations. His mother was only fourteen when she had him. And like most single mothers at the time, she gave birth to Johnny in a home for unwed mothers run by the Grey Nuns. The price to pay for bearing a child in sin was to give birth in an auditorium full of Université Laval medical students, who all clapped wildly if the delivery was a success. His mother used to say it was probably at that exact moment that her son was bitten by the showbiz bug.

Apartment 6 was where the Nolet family lived. Mr. Nolet was a chartered accountant who worked for the Ministry of Finance. He had six children from a first marriage, and during a trade mission to London he met a charming young girl on Carnaby Street, in a miniskirt and sporting the latest hairdo, by the name of Nancy Pickford. It was love at first sight. They got married in a little Catholic church in Brixton, in south London. She changed her name to Nancy Nolet, which always sounded a little odd. She got the shock of her life when she arrived in Quebec City. First because she didn't speak a word of French, and second because overnight she became a mother of six. But she valued her freedom too much to just be a housewife, so she got herself a job as a waitress in the tearoom at the Château Frontenac, where they served afternoon tea in the best of British tradition, complete with crumpets and scones and cucumber sandwiches. And the good ladies of Grande Allée loved having tea served to them by a waitress with a British accent, as they could imagine they were having high tea in high fashion in Highgate. Of course she was very disillusioned with her new life in Quebec so she'd come home late at night, often inebriated, and her husband would be waiting up to give her hell. We were often treated to their memorable domestic scenes which might last until the wee hours of the morning.

So as you can see, 887 Murray Avenue was really very representative of Quebec at the time: about 80 percent francophone, 20 percent anglophone, still very few immigrants, and as many people leaning right as there were leaning left.

PARC DES BRAVES NO. 1

*Robert spins the building back to its original position, but now
projected on the screen is a video shot of Parc des Braves in
the foreground with the Lower Town and the Laurentians in
the background. Simultaneously, a model of the park entrance
(with the Monument des Braves in the middle, the two
pavilions on each side and the long balustrade between them)
silently slides out and stops in front of the screen, exactly
its width.*

Diving deep in the waters of my past
   I see this one bright place from far away;
The first and oldest memory of them all
   is what began my lifelong one-act play.

The Parc des Braves, that legendary place
   where every Sunday wealthy families go
To eat their picnics sitting on the cliff,
   gazing at the town stretched out below.

The day my family moves to Upper Town,
   my father rushes to bring us to the park
While my mother, always dutiful and meek,
   unpacks boxes until long after dark.

My father has a war vet's pension, and
   now as well, a taxi driver's pay.
He never dreamed his life would look so good
   as it did in Parc des Braves on that spring day.

He points to Lower Town, our former home,
   where the working classes live in the crowded streets
Of Saint-Sauveur, Saint-Roch, and Limoilou,
   and people work like dogs to make ends meet.

I can see our silhouettes as children now;
   the sun goes down and the afternoon gets colder,
My brother Dave, and sisters Ann and Lynda,
   and I ride on my hero's trusty shoulders.

The model of the park entrance slides offstage.

STREET NAMES

Using his cellphone again, Robert makes a world map appear on the screen and zooms in on the Montcalm district, satellite view, showing the street names and places of interest.

We lived here. Right in the heart of the Montcalm district, an area sandwiched between two battlefields that were pivotal in the history of Canada: the Parc des Braves, to the north, and the Plains of Abraham, to the south. That's why the streets in this neighbourhood are almost all named after the great British and French military officers.

This is what's called historical toponymy (or the historical naming of places). In theory, when you come across a street called Murray, it's supposed to bring to mind General James Murray (*projects portrait of Murray*), who was Quebec's first British governor. Murray fought alongside James Wolfe (*a portrait of Wolfe appears next to Murray's*) at the famous Battle of the Plains of Abraham. Since Wolfe fell very early on in the battle, Murray took command of the British troops and managed to get the French troops under Montcalm to surrender.

But just between you and me, it probably wasn't a very hard battle to win, judging by this painting by Hervey Smythe (*projects painting by Smythe*); the French troops, you can see them here in blue, were clearly outnumbered by the British troops, in red, who had reinforcements coming from all the way down beyond the Beauport Flats.

And in fact that was General Wolfe's strategy, to scale the cliffs of the Plains of Abraham after landing his troops here, at Anse au Foulon. So this is another memory-place: when you hear "Anse au Foulon" it's supposed to trigger the memory of that very important historical event.

ANSE AU FOULON

In my case, it triggers something else entirely.

Projection of a period photo of the beach at Anse au Foulon.

When I think of Anse au Foulon, I think of the
beautiful sandy beach it was to become centuries later,
and where my father worked as a lifeguard in the
1930s.

Photo of Robert's father, on the beach.

Here he is, barely twenty years old, in his bathing suit,
with his lifeguard's hat and his St. Michael's
Medal — St. Michael is the patron saint of lifeguards.

Photo of his father on the beach doing a handstand.

My father spent most of his youth at Anse au Foulon
in a poor neighbourhood called Cap-Blanc. During

the Great Depression, families would take their kids out of school and send them to work. My father was only eight years old when he was sent to the docks to work on the boats so he could help his family.

Photo of his father in swimming trunks, cigarette in hand.

In those days they didn't pay children with money, they paid them with flour or packs of cigarettes. My father smoked from the age of eight until he was seventy-five, when he died of lung cancer.

Photo of his father, bearded, in his navy uniform.

When the Second World War broke out, it was only natural for him to join the Canadian Navy because he was used to working on boats. He had all kinds of adventures. He was decorated several times. But we never really got to know the details of his exploits, because my father was a man of few words, and also because one of his great qualities was his remarkable humility.

Wedding photo of Robert's parents after the ceremony, on the church steps.

After the war, my father met my mother, a young woman from the Saint-Roch district, where they got married. My mother's sisters were all very jealous. They said my mother didn't deserve my father because, according to them, he was the best-looking guy in the whole city.

Photo of Robert's father in his taxi driver's uniform.

When my father left the navy, he had to find a civilian job. As he could barely read or write, the only job he could find was driving a taxi. But the great advantage he had over the other cabbies was that he was perfectly bilingual, as he'd learned English during his years in the navy. That meant he could offer sightseeing tours to American tourists, who usually rewarded him with very generous tips.

Photo of his father with Ann, Dave, and Robert in his arms.

So for me, as a kid, my father was the ultimate superhero: a good-looking, strong, athletic man who had saved many lives when he was young, who had risked his own life during the war, and who was now prepared to make any sacrifice at all to give his children the best possible standard of living.

THE LIBRARY

With a swipe of his cellphone, Robert slides the photo off the screen and dials a number while taking off his jacket. Meanwhile, the screen/wall revolves and the front of 887 Murray reappears but then rotates another 90 degrees. The other side of the building is now a wall of bookshelves, his present-day personal library. At the same time, a floor lamp with a tray table glides on stage left and moves over to far stage right. We hear a voicemail greeting.

"Your message has been transferred to a voice messaging system. 'Fred' cannot take your call at the moment. At the tone, please leave a message."*

A beep indicating the beginning of the recording.

Hi Fred, Robert Lepage here. Listen, old pal, long time no see. Sorry to call you on your private number – I

---

* The passages in grey are performed in French, with the translation in surtitles.

guess it's your cell number. It's just that I didn't have a work number or a home number for you. By chance I ran into Marie-Christine the other day at the mall and she gave me your private number. I promise I won't give it to anyone . . .

Beep indicating the end of the recording.

Hold on . . . that was way too quick!

To the audience:

Fred is a guy I studied with at the Conservatoire d'art dramatique, Quebec city's theatre school, many years ago. Let's just say he wasn't the greatest actor, but he had a fabulous voice.

He touches automatic redial on his cellphone.

So he was the first in our class to find a job after leaving the Conservatoire. Radio-Canada hired him as a newsreader at our local TV station. He was raking in the bucks, and we were all dead jealous because we were starving artists. But recently I've heard that he has some pretty serious financial problems.

Beep, beginning of recording.

Geez, Fred, you don't leave people much time to leave a message. I'll try to be brief.

I need your services as a coach to learn a text that's a bit tricky. I remember at the Conservatoire you always had really good mnemonic tricks for memorizing those great long passages by Shakespeare and Racine. Obviously I'm not asking you to do it for nothing, I'll remunerate you, we just have to agree on a price.

Beep, end of recording.

Damn!

To the audience:

The problem was he was making so much money that he started partying and boozing a lot, so his face started to swell up. Radio-Canada didn't find him so telegenic anymore, so they did what they always do in those situations: they sent him to work in radio.

He calls again.

For years he had his own weekly show. But I have the feeling they must have sacked him because I haven't heard him for at least three months.

Beep, start of recording.

Yeah, Fred! You know what, I'll just leave my number, and when you get this message, you call me back. How about we do that, it'll be way simpler.

Now if I could only remember my own number!
Listen, I'll hang up, because I'm gonna have to go into
my contacts to try to find it, then I'll call you again
and leave it on your voicemail, then you call me when
you can.

Okay so we'll do that then! Ciao.

He hangs up.

God, this is so complicated!

Robert looks for his number on his cellphone.

Right. (418) 262-3258.

3, 2, 5, 8 . . . How am I going to remember 3, 2, 5, 8?

3 plus 2 equals 5. So 3, 2, 5.

2 plus 5 equals 8. No! Wait a minute, 2 plus 5 is 7.

So I take the 3, skip over the 2 and add it to the 5, and
that gives me 8.

He calls again.

If I can still remember my trick!

To the audience:

Not only is my memory shot, but I'm lousy at math too.

Beep, then recorded message.

"I'm sorry. This mailbox is full. Goodbye!"

To the audience:

Sometimes, I get the impression it's my own brain that has storage-capacity problems. In the last few years I've had so much information in my head and things to remember that I just can't store any more new information. I have the feeling my head is crammed as full as the shelves in my library.

Picks up a book from the tray table of the floor lamp.

I mean, if I had to decide where to file the complete works of Michèle Lalonde in my personal library, I have to admit I'd be in trouble, because not only do I have no more space, but even if I did, I don't have a "Quebec contemporary poetry" section. And even if I did, it wouldn't do her justice, because Michèle Lalonde didn't only write poetry, she wrote prose, novels, plays, and political essays. And her writings don't just relate to Quebec, they're universal.

Obviously, if this were a public library, I'd simply file her writings under "L" for Lalonde. But unfortunately a personal library is somewhat like a personal memory, it's not arranged in alphabetical order. It works by association. In theory, every personal library should reflect the mental organization of its owner, not just in the choice of books, but also in the whole complex network of associations related to those choices.

So if I want to be able to locate the book with "Speak White" in it, I'd have to file it somewhere between Pierre Vallière's *Nègres blancs d'Amérique* and a collection of poetry by Jacques Brault. But to do that, I'd have to undo my whole complicated system of book associations and I'd be completely lost.

He replaces the book on the tray table.

This was exactly the kind of chaos and confusion that struck my family in 1961 when my paternal grandmother came to live with us. She was starting to show the first symptoms of Alzheimer's disease. My father swore up and down that he'd never put her in a home, and that he'd look after her until she died. A very noble intention, but there wasn't enough room in our home for a seventh person.

He takes a panel out of the left side of the bookshelf, revealing a side view of the living room of the apartment at 887 Murray. His grandmother enters the apartment, walking slowly with a cane. She crosses the living room and goes down the hallway towards the other rooms.

When we had visitors, we'd have them sleep on the living room sofa. That was fine for a girl of fourteen, but not for a seventy-five-year-old lady.

Robert pulls out the next panel of the bookshelf, this time revealing his parents' bedroom. The bedroom door opens, the grandmother takes a look but doesn't go in and instead carries on down the hall.

Obviously there was no way my mother was going to sleep in the same room as her mother-in-law, with whom she didn't get on that well. As it was, my mother was always complaining she didn't have enough private time with my father.

He pulls out a third panel, revealing the girls' room. Same thing. The door opens, the grandmother takes a look and then carries on.

No way she could sleep in the girls' room either, because she terrified my little sister Lynda and my big sister Ann said my grandmother was "smelly."

He skips the fourth panel and pulls out the fifth and last panel, revealing the kitchen.

And as we certainly weren't going to ask her to sleep in the kitchen, the solution my parents came up with was to reassign the boys' room . . .

He pulls out the fourth section, revealing the boys' room. As he explains the new configuration, Robert moves toy figures of Dave and Lynda and trades the bunk bed in the boys' room for one of the girls' single beds.

... so my brother Dave sleeps on the living room sofa, I share the bunk bed with my sister Lynda, and she gives up her bed to my grandmother.

The grandmother appears in the doorway of the boys' room, which is going to be hers.

At the time this seemed to us the most sensible solution, but in fact it didn't suit anybody. My brother complained nonstop that we were watching TV in "his" room. My mother couldn't sleep anymore because my brother watched TV until late at night, and my sister Ann complained she had become a permanent unpaid babysitter. As for me, I spent the first eight years of my life sharing a bedroom with my two sisters, which probably explains a lot.

Even my grandmother, who had a room of her own, never really felt at home. The worse her symptoms got, the more she wanted to run away. That was just about manageable during the daytime but at night, sadly, we often had to lock her in her bedroom.

He rolls down a blind over the bookshelves.

TAXI AT NIGHT NO. 1

Night lighting. The building turns 45 degrees counterclockwise and stops at an angle so the side and back face the audience.

Costs go up when my grandmother comes to stay,
    as now we have another mouth to feed.
My weary father takes on extra hours
    and drives at night to pay for all our needs.

While he speaks, a model of the father's black taxi (to scale with the building), with headlights and roof light on, drives on stage right and parks behind the building.

In the early hours of morning he comes home;
    he pulls up in the yard and parks the car.
However many times he counts his tips,
    he knows that they won't get us very far.

He pulls a pack of cigarettes from his coat;
    a glow of red appears against the black.

He takes a drag to slow the rush of time
    and ease the weight of boredom off his back.

The radio in his taxi cab is on;
    he winds the windows up and settles in.
A cloud of cigarette smoke gathers round;
    the city sleeps, his showtime can begin.

The layer of sky that sends back radio waves
    is higher up at night than in the day;
So now the signals bounce across the border,
    and my father's favourite songs begin to play.

It is a strange and private symphony,
    the rumble of the motor, like a mantra,
The static of the far-off radio stations,
    and the steamy, sultry voice of Nancy Sinatra.

*"Bang Bang" plays, sung by Nancy Sinatra. Robert crouches
down to listen to the first verse. The volume goes down when
he starts speaking again.*

My father learned by heart these future hits,
    from Baltimore, Detroit and Chicago —
A far cry from the Elvis imitations
    of our local pop star Johnny Farago.

The signal also reaches Montreal,
    and right away the music companies
Record the stolen songs in Quebec French
    and never pay a cent in royalties.

My father wonders, lighting another smoke,
    if we can catch their airwaves, can they ours?
What must they think, to hear their songs come back,
    like odd cross-pollinated flowers?

As the song ends, the taxi starts up again and exits stage left.
As the building rotates another 45 degrees so that the back faces
the audience, Robert opens it up, as if opening French doors, to
reveal a full-scale ultramodern kitchen inside. The folded-back
doors on each side now suggest a vestibule (light switches and a
thermostat on the left, Japanese calligraphy wallhanging and a
closet on the right).

REHEARSAL COACH

Robert takes off his vest and drops it carelessly in the closet. He rolls up his sleeves, turns on the kitchen lights, sits at the counter on a stool, puts on his glasses, and looks at a three-page document.

The doorbell rings. He exits stage right and stays out of sight.

Hi Fred, how are you? Come in, come on in! No, no, you can keep your boots on. But let me take your coat. I'll put it in the closet.

Robert enters again, carrying a coat. Throughout their conversation, Robert's expression, gestures and tone evoke his invisible visitor (the ellipses between Robert's lines indicate when Fred is speaking).

Did you have trouble finding the place?

. . .

Yeah I know . . . since they merged the suburbs with
the city, they've changed the names of the streets.
Before, this was Boulevard Bastien and it went all the
way up to the Huron village. But they changed it to
Boulevard Louis-XIV. Don't ask me why.

Robert hangs Fred's coat in the closet. As he goes back into the
kitchen, the building rotates 90 degrees to a side view of the
kitchen. Frosted glass cabinets, a stainless-steel fridge,
adjoining counter with a kettle, microwave, etc. along the back
wall. There's another stool in front of an island with a sink and
tap at one end. Robert is moving around behind this island
throughout the scene.

The problem is, the taxi drivers haven't updated their
GPS data so you ask them to take you three blocks and
they take you three times around town. Come, let's go
sit in the kitchen.

Robert opens the fridge, addressing Fred sitting at the island.

Can I get you something to drink?

. . .

I've got all kinds of things. I've got beer, I've got white
wine. Unless you want me to make you something
stronger, a gin and tonic or a dry martini . . .

. . .

Ah . . . you don't drink anymore? Really?

. . .

Oh . . . It's just that . . . I don't know . . . It's weird to think of you without a glass in your hand . . .

. . .

No, no, that's not what I meant, at all . . . Don't take it like that . . .

I have other things, if you like. I've got juice, mineral water . . . Or do you want me to make you a coffee?

Closes fridge.

No, I know . . . I'll make you a rooibos tea. It's very good, you'll see, and it's very trendy these days, everyone's drinking it. It's supposed to be great for your health. Especially if you're in detox . . . It'll clean up your liver.

As he talks, Robert makes tea for Fred and sets down a mug and milk jug in front of him.

Why did you quit drinking? Did you have health problems?

. . .

For sure, decent red wine isn't cheap.

Especially when you have money troubles . . . that can't be easy.

. . .

Where are you doing your detox? In a private clinic, or are social services paying for it?

. . .

Why would you need two treatments? Isn't one usually enough?

. . .

Oh, cocaine as well? I didn't know . . .

. . .

Well, I mean . . . we all knew . . . At least I knew you had a drinking problem but I didn't know you had problems with recreational drugs as well.

But do you still have your job at Radio-Canada?

. . .

I hadn't heard you on the radio for ages, so I thought you must have got laid off, with all those cuts at

Radio-Canada . . . so many people have lost their jobs in the last little while.

Do you take milk?

. . .

But if you don't have your weekly show anymore, what have they got you doing? Working in the archives?

. . .

And how do you feel about that? It doesn't bother you to be working in the cafeteria?

. . .

No but . . . you just said you're in charge of the cold cuts.

. . .

Oh okay, I get it, those obituaries . . . that are cooked up in advance. Like when a politician dies, and they do a story on his life that you think must have been put together that very day, but in fact it was already in the can years before.

. . .

So your job is to freshen up the cold cuts, is that it?

. . .

So you're the one who narrates them? It must be interesting.

. . .

In fact I always wondered about that . . . So are cold cuts just for politicians, or do you do them for other, you know . . . public figures too? People in the culture business, for example . . .

. . .

Oh for sure, Céline Dion, she must have had a cold cut ready for her since she was twelve!

Anyway, they'll never use it. It said in *Paris Match* last week that Céline was eternal.

. . .

No, I was thinking more, like . . . small-time local talent?

. . .

Well, I mean, people like . . . well, say, me, for example . . . Will I have the honour of my own cold cut one day, or do I have to wait until I've accomplished something big?

. . .

How do you know that?

. . .

Were you the one who recorded it?

. . .

I see, and, uh . . . what does it say? What I mean is . . .
did it seem fair and impartial or . . .

. . .

Well, of course you can't remember every single cold
cut you've done.

But someone like me who has a cold cut . . . Say I
wanted to go to Radio-Canada to . . . to consult it . . .
and check that none of the information is incorrect . . .

. . .

Yes, I understand that. But you . . . do *you* have access
to them?

. . .

So what if I went with you?

. . .

Yes, but if I gave you some money? Would you be able to get it out for me, on an old DVD or something?

The kettle boils.

. . .

No, I understand. I certainly wouldn't want to jeopardize what's left of your job at Radio-Canada.

. . .

What's that?

. . .

Yeah yeah, I heard it. No, no . . . I'm not . . .

He turns off the kettle and pours water into Fred's mug.

So, as I was explaining on the phone, it's Michèle Lalonde's "Speak White."

He puts down the pages in front of Fred.

I don't know if it's the particular form of the poem that makes it so difficult to memorize . . . you know, it was in that wonderful era when Quebec poets felt they had to experiment with form . . . the Automatiste period . . . so no way it's going to rhyme. It would have been a piece of cake to remember if it rhymed. At least if it rhymed, I'd have something to grab hold of. But it doesn't rhyme, and that's that . . . I can't pretend it does. What doesn't rhyme doesn't rhyme.

. . .

What's that?

. . .

No no, I know a few bits. I might be old enough for a cold cut but I'm not completely soft in the head. I can still learn things by heart . . .

. . .

Anyway, you be the judge of that . . . There are three pages of it . . . Let's start and then if I get stuck . . . you help me out . . .

. . .

Do you take sugar?

. . .

"Speak white . . .

so nice it is to hear you

speak of Lost Paradise"

. . .

What?

. . .

What did I say?

. . .

I said Lost Paradise?

. . .

No, I know. I always get it backwards . . .

. . .

I dunno . . . I always think of *Lost Horizon* . . .

. . .

No, that's David Lynch . . . *Lost Highway* is David
Lynch. *Lost Horizon* is Frank Capra. But *Paradise
Lost* . . . The thing is I have to get into the habit of
saying it . . .

. . .

It's that long epic poem by Milton about the creation
of the world . . . About the Fall of Adam and Eve . . . in
the Garden of Eden . . . you've never read that, huh?

. . .

Yeah, I know. I don't even know why I asked you. I
didn't think you'd have read it. Anyway, it's *Paradise
Lost* . . .

"so nice it is to hear you speak of Paradise Lost
or of the graceful, elusive figure . . ."

Graceful elusive? Or elusive graceful?

. . .

Graceful elusive. I got it the first time, but I just wasn't
sure.

"or of the graceful, elusive figure trembling

in Shakespeare's sonnets . . ."

. . .

What's that?

. . .

It's because in Shakespeare's sonnets . . . at least,

according to the experts . . . the first half of the
sonnets are very obviously addressed to a young
woman, but the other half . . . are somewhat
ambiguous. They were most likely addressed to a
young man. That's maybe why Michèle Lalonde writes
"the graceful, elusive figure trembling in Shakespeare's
sonnets."

. . .

Well, yeah. Exactly. You see . . . it seems Shakespeare
swung both ways too, apparently . . . Well, you know,
those theatre people . . . everyone knows they're a
wicked bunch, not the same as media people . . . They
like exploring, they like to experiment!

. . .

That really has nothing to do with it . . . Look, it's
always like this! I've got like a mental blockage . . . It's
like I'm trying to catch a greased pig with my bare
hands.

Okay . . . I'm gonna try and concentrate.

"We are an ignorant and . . ."

. . .

No, don't tell me. "We are an ignorant and . . .

. . .

DON'T TELL ME!

. . .

"We are an ignorant and . . ."

Long silence.

Okay, what is it?

. . .

Ignorant and what?

. . .

An ignorant and inarticulate people? Geez, this is
going great . . .

"we are an ignorant and stammering people

but not deaf to the genius of a language

so speak with the accent of—"

. . . and then there are four of them and I never know
what order they come in. There's Byron, there's Keats,
there's Shelley, there's Milton . . .

. . .

Milton, Byron, Shelley, and Keats?

. . .

Milton, Byron, Shelley, and Keats. Fine, but how am I going to remember Milton, Byron, Shelley and Keats? There's no good reason why they're in that order. No chronological, historical or alphabetical reason why on earth they're in that order . . .

. . .

MBSK? Milton, Byron, Shelley, Keats. I guess so, but how am I gonna remember MBSK? I'll need to find a mnemonic trick to remember MBSK. What about "My Beautiful Sashimi of Kyoto"? Okay, so that might make me think of MBSK, which might then remind me of Milton, Byron, Shelley, and Keats? Is that it?

. . .

Oh sure, "it works." No, it does not work!!! Because poetry doesn't work like that! Poetry takes a visceral memory, it has to come from your gut. You can't be thinking about mnemonic tricks, like the first letter, then the second letter, which reminds you of the third letter . . .

. . .

Look, I do appreciate your suggestion. It's not your fault. It's just that in this case, it doesn't apply. Let's put it that way. It doesn't apply.

Anyway . . . how about . . . we call it a day? This obviously isn't gonna work.

. . .

No no, it's not your fault. It's me, I can't concentrate. There are days like that . . . when you can't focus. Hasn't it ever happened to you, that you had trouble focusing?

. . .

There!

He takes a beer out of the fridge.

. . .

Well, actually, yes! It *is* your fault because you're the one who went and put those goddam cold cuts in my head. For the past ten minutes I haven't been able to think about anything else and now I'm obsessed. I know it's immature of me, but I can't help it . . . It bugs me, thinking about how people will remember me when I'm not around anymore. I'm just realizing it right now, I do care!

Because you've just informed me that there's someone, somewhere at Radio-Canada, who has decided what the value of my contribution to Quebec's cultural heritage is, and there's not a thing I can do to change that. Now it'll be hanging over my head like a sword of Damocles, it'll haunt me all my life. I know it! I know what I'm like! I can just feel it!

. . .

I'm sorry, but I think what a person leaves behind them is important.

. . .

It's like Boulevard Bastien, which was named in honour of one of the great Aboriginal families of the Quebec city region. And then we use municipal mergers as an excuse to get rid of the Indians and replace them with a king of France. Since when did you hear that Louis XIV lived in a bungalow in Charlesbourg?

It's like in Montreal, they have Robert Gravel *Lane*, and Pauline Julien *Cul-de-Sac*! I tell you, it's really worthwhile to spend your whole life fighting to awaken the social and political consciousness of the Québécois people only to end up as a cul-de-sac in Rosemont! She never lived there, she wasn't even born there! Everyone knows perfectly well she lived on Carré Saint-Louis, right opposite where the great poet

Émile Nelligan lived. And explain something else to me, will you? Why has Carré Saint-Louis never been renamed Carré Émile Nelligan? Is that how the collective memory of Quebecers works? Is that how we remember people who made an important contribution to our cultural heritage!?!

. . .

Yes! Of course you don't give a damn. Because one thing's for sure: there won't be a single street in Quebec named after you. So it's easy for you to say!

The kitchen rotates 90 degrees back to its original position. Robert comes out of the kitchen and stands facing stage left.

Where are you going?

Fred! FRED! Where are you going? Don't be such a baby! It was a joke! It was a bad joke, I know, I'm not a stand-up comic!

. . .

Geez, you're so touchy!

. . .

Come on back . . . shut the door and let's start again . . . We'll go back in the kitchen, I'll really concentrate this time and we'll get there.

Goes to take Fred's coat out of the closet.

No, no . . . That, I never said . . .

. . .

Well if that's how you want to take it!

. . .

Wait! I said I'd pay you, so I'll pay you. There.

We said twenty dollars an hour. Let's say we worked for two hours.

. . .

I know we didn't even do ten minutes. But a paid debt is a friend kept, as they say. Here, I'll add another ten. Give a good tip to the cabbie.

. . .

Take it! My god, don't be so huffy! I've never seen anyone so proud!

He puts the bills in the pockets of the coat.

. . .

What the hell's the matter with you? Did your sense of humour get lost in the drunk tank, or what? Do you think it'll come back one day?

. . .

Well, fine then! Get out! You think I'm gonna stand here and take your insults!

Robert throws Fred's coat at him. Fred leaves. Robert goes back into the kitchen, picks up "Speak White" and sits down to memorize it. He takes such an angry swig of his beer that it spills all over his shirt.

Shit!

As he's rehearsing, he takes off the shirt and puts on a clean one from the closet. Then he closes the kitchen doors, which become the rear of the building again.

"We are an . . ." What is it again? Ignorant . . . "We are an ignorant . . ." Ignorant and what? Ignorant and stammering . . . "We are an ignorant and stammering people . . ." Ignorant and stammering . . . "We are an arrogant . . ." No, we're not arrogant, dammit, we're ignorant . . . "We are an ignorant and stammering people . . ." We are an ignorant and stammering people . . . "We are an ignorant and stammering people . . ."

FLQ – THE MONSTER OF PONT-ROUGE

Night. Rear wall of 887. A large, blue steel drum with a wooden lid glides on stage left.

A full-length lifesize black-and-white photo of Donald Gordon is projected on the central column of the rear wall.

In 1962, Donald Gordon, President and CEO of the Canadian National Railway, is summoned to appear before a parliamentary commission in Ottawa. He's asked to explain why, out of the company's seventeen vice-presidents across Canada, not one of them speaks French, and he replies, cool as a cucumber, that such appointments are based on merit, and that unfortunately French Canadians don't have the skills to fill these positions. As you can imagine, his statement triggers outrage among Quebec's francophones.

Projection of the Wolfe Monument intact, then with the top knocked off.

A few weeks later, on the Plains of Abraham, the monument to General Wolfe is knocked down.

Not far from there, a serial killer is prowling around in the woods.

Projection of photo of Léopold Dion.

Léopold Dion pretends to be a photographer for an American magazine devoted to the male body. His victims are young boys between the ages of eight and thirteen. He lures them into his car, drives them out of town, tells them to undress, takes pictures of them with a camera that doesn't even have any film in it, then rapes them, strangles them and buries them.

My brother Dave is only twelve at the time, and he earns a bit of pocket money by delivering papers in our neighbourhood. My mother decides that from now on she'll go with him on his paper route, which he finds deeply humiliating. And so that my sister Lynda and I won't have to stay home alone, she asks Mrs. Côté, our neighbour in Apartment 1, to look after us while she's out.

Robert picks up a string of firecrackers that was lying in the shadows on the back stoop of the building.

For the next few months I'm condemned to playing outside with the rowdy Gorilla boys, whose idea of fun is lighting jumbo firecrackers in the garbage cans in the back alley.

Meanwhile, Montreal is witnessing the birth of the FLQ, the Front de libération du Québec.

An animated projection of the letters "FLQ" appears on the wall in red, as though someone is spray-painting graffiti. Meanwhile Robert lights the fuse.

In the next four months, more than thirty bomb attacks are perpetrated against federal buildings, military barracks and mailboxes in Montreal's wealthy Westmount neighbourhood.

Robert drops the firecrackers into the steel drum, claps down the lid and holds it tight. Light and smoke escape around the edges. Sound of explosions. The fresh paint of the letters "FLQ" drips down the wall like blood.

It all culminates in Quebec city when a statue of Queen Victoria is blown up in broad daylight.

Projection of statue of Queen Victoria. Lights in apartments go on and off, sounds of explosion and broken glass.

The blast is so powerful you can hear it all over the city. But if you talk to people who lived in Quebec city at the time, very few remember the event, and even fewer remember that there was ever a statue of Queen Victoria there.

It's what they call a collective memory lapse.

Because while in Montreal the papers are plastered with news of the FLQ attacks . . .

Projection of the front page of Montréal-Matin: *"LE FLQ EN BLOC!"*

. . . all the Quebec city papers are talking about is the discovery of the bodies of Léopold Dion's victims.

Projection of front page of Quebec city's Le Soleil *newspaper: "Découverte des corps des 3 jeunes Québécois disparus."*

At the time of his arrest, he admits to having killed the three young boys. But more than fifty unresolved cases in the Quebec city area would be later attributed to him.

Blackout.

CHRISTMAS 1963

Robert enters stage right pushing a trolley loaded with five cardboard boxes.

What you see here are all our family mementos, carefully packed away in boxes by my sister Lynda, who over time became in a way the repository of all the family memories. There are all kinds of things in here: photo albums, tape recordings, videos, even a few Super 8 movies. As they're perishable items, my sister asked me if I could get them digitized.

Takes out his cellphone.

To my amazement, all this stuff barely takes up one percent of this little gadget's memory. All that's missing is the smell.

He starts filming with his cellphone, and the film is instantly projected on a large screen behind him. First he films the top of a box on which is handwritten "NOËLS."

For example, in this box here are all the Christmas mementos. It says Noëls with an "s" because they're from ALL the Christmases we spent as a family.

He swings the trolley around 180 degrees, still filming. The backs of the five boxes are now his Uncle Maurice's house and garage, like a doll's house. A long sequence shot follows everything he describes, perfectly reproduced using little figurines, furniture, toy cars, etc.

But my favourite Christmas of all was never documented. It was the one I spent in Château-d'Eau, at my Uncle Maurice and Aunt Jeanne's house, in 1963.

My uncle and aunt never had children, so when Christmastime came around they borrowed other people's kids. That year, my sister Lynda and I were the lucky ones.

When we arrived at the house, I was struck by the fact that they each had their own car parked in the garage. Which was really unusual at the time. My father didn't even have his own car; he'd had to borrow one from the taxi company to drive us there.

This is my Aunt Jeanne, my mother's eldest sister. She was a really fabulous cook. When you walked in the house it smelled like you were walking into a bakery. My uncle had kitted her out with the fanciest kitchen gadgets I'd ever seen. My mother might have married

the best-looking guy, but my aunt had definitely
snagged the richest.

*The camera pans over the box without a lid, which is the living
room.*

Christmas at Château-d'Eau was like stepping into an
American Christmas movie, with all the same clichés:
the big Christmas tree all lit up, a stack of gifts
underneath, the little black cat in the corner called
Noireau, Fido the faithful dog, the Christmas
stockings hanging from the mantelpiece.

But what impressed me most was that they had two
floors.

*He opens the lid of the box labelled "NOËLS," revealing the
master bedroom.*

There was a huge staircase that led up to the master
bedroom, which had been meticulously decorated and
furnished with antiques they'd had shipped over from
Europe.

I couldn't help but notice that my uncle and aunt
didn't sleep in the same bed. I was still far too young
for anyone to have told me about the birds and the
bees . . . but I had a hunch that this probably had a lot
to do with the fact that they'd never had children.

He opens the lid of the last box.

Then there was this giant bathroom where my sister Lynda would spend hours and hours counting the tiles and admiring the ceramics. Here she is on the toilet, pretending to be the Queen of France sitting on her throne in the Hall of Mirrors at Versailles. My aunt even nicknamed her "Marie en Toilette." My sister always had a thing for plumbing and pipes and whatnot. Which could explain why, years later, she became a secretary for a big waterworks and sewage systems company.

On the night of the 24th, it was clear that my uncle and aunt didn't believe either in Santa Claus or in the baby Jesus. So no midnight mass, but that didn't stop them from getting us out of bed and taking us down to the living room to open our presents.

Back to the front of the house. Robert opens the French doors of the living room and positions his cellphone in the box such that we can see the figurine of his uncle and his own gigantic face in the doorway.

This is my Uncle Maurice. He was a very well-regarded lawyer who worked on Parliament Hill as a legal advisor to the government. He had noticed my interest in everything miniature: Meccano, scale models, Lego. He asked me if one day I wanted to be an architect. I don't think I even knew what the word meant, but to please him I said yes. He said, "Then you'll have to persuade your parents to send you to a private school. Because if they keep sending you to public school, you'll never become an architect and you'll never live in a nice house like this."

Then he gave me the Christmas present he'd picked out specially for me.

Robert puts his hand through the doorway into the living room and takes a tiny gift from under the tree. He unwraps it using one hand. He sets the model car, tinier than a thimble, on the tip of his middle finger in front of the figure of his uncle, as if his uncle were holding it out to him.

It was a model Lincoln. I'd never seen one before so I asked him, "What's a Lincoln?" And he said, "It's a car that very important people ride in."

Projection fades to black.

LINCOLN

The apartments light up as the building revolves 180 degrees counterclockwise. The left side of the building is open to reveal the Lepage living room. A photo of Abraham Lincoln appears on the screen of an old black-and-white TV.

The Lincoln was named after the sixteenth president of the United States, Abraham Lincoln, who is still considered the greatest American president of all time. It was Lincoln who ended the Civil War, restored the Union, and most important of all, abolished slavery.

Incidentally, the expression "speak white" comes from those days, in the cotton fields. The plantation owners were afraid of slave rebellions, and forbade the slaves to speak creole. They told them to "speak white", meaning speak like the Whites.

Robert picks up a toy Lincoln from among the other toys on the floor and turns the channel knob on the TV. We see the famous archival footage of the assassination of JFK in Dallas.

In the 1960s the Lincoln became the official car of the U.S. presidents. In fact it was in a car exactly like this one that John F. Kennedy was assassinated in 1963.

He changes the channel again. Archival footage of Queen Elizabeth's visit to Quebec city.

It was also in a Lincoln like this one that Queen Elizabeth II rode through the streets of Quebec city in 1964.

I remember it well because my father took us to Grande Allée for the occasion, and people turned their backs to her when she went by.

Change of channel again. Archival footage of the events he describes.

While he's talking, Robert takes off his pants, under which are pyjama bottoms. A huge chair and TV in the living room suggest Robert as a child of seven or eight.

The night before, at the Centre Durocher in the Lower Town, there had been a huge rally for Quebec independence led by Pierre Bourgault, who happened to be a great friend of my Uncle Maurice's.

People were gearing up that night for a big demonstration the next day on the Plains of Abraham near the Citadel, where the Queen was staying. To deal with the 680 or so demonstrators, the forces of law and order deployed more than 4,000 policemen armed with their *matraques,* or truncheons, who beat people indiscriminately. That day is still remembered as *Samedi de la matraque,* or Truncheon Saturday.

Change of channel. Archival footage of a full-out hockey brawl.

Robert, now sitting on the floor in front of the TV, is setting up a chessboard. As he talks, the black pieces appear to represent the federalist camp and his father; the white pieces, the separatist camp and his mother.

Up to that point in Quebec, the politics were quite simple: people either voted red or they voted blue. Red for the Liberal Party and blue for the very conservative Union Nationale. But after Truncheon Saturday, you had to choose sides — you were either federalist or separatist.

My father, who had fought for the Queen in the armed forces, was naturally federalist. But my mother had begun to show some sympathy for the separatist movement. My father decided that from that point on, when we had the choice, we would watch certain TV shows in English.

He changes channel to the same hockey game, but this time in English.

He finishes setting up the chessboard. Still in the living room, he rolls down the blind behind him.

AFTERNOON TEA AT THE CHÂTEAU FRONTENAC

The building rotates 180 degrees to show the projector screen wall.

An old black-and-white short entitled Afternoon Tea at the Hôtel Château Frontenac. Wide-angle view of a large room with high ceilings, sumptuously decorated, where tea is being served.

There's no dialogue, only ambient sound consisting of muted conversations, the tinkle of silver spoons in fine porcelain cups and music played by a small ensemble dressed in wigs and period costumes.

The camera pans the room showing mostly very old, elegant clients (bow ties, fur coats, fur hats, jewellery) sitting at tables, and serving staff (headwaiter in a tuxedo, waitresses in shirt-dresses and white caps).

The camera lingers on a waitress who brings to mind Nancy Nolet.

Medium shot of two old ladies at a table. One lights a cigarette, the other dips her napkin into her glass of water and rubs at a spot on her dress.

Shot of two more old ladies: one holds out the sugarbowl, the other drops four lumps in her tea and adds milk. The music ends and her companion claps, cigarette in mouth.

Blackout.

PURGATORY

The building rotates to face the audience.

A figure on the top-left balcony, Mrs. Robson, is washing her living room window, her arm moving back and forth.

On the balcony below, the figure of Robert's mother sits smoking a cigarette, the smoke spirals upwards.

At the main entrance is a figure of a man in a grey suit wearing a fedora and carrying a suitcase.

Robert enters stage left and stops in front of the building.

> The husband went to work and the wife stayed home;
>   that was how it was, back in those years.
> The children were at school the whole day long,
>   leaving my mother alone and bored to tears.
>
> Thank God for door-to-door salesmen passing by,
>   who fanned the flames of passion in our block;

They knew their profits came from lonely housewives,
    and they broke some hearts with their good looks
    and talk.

Robert picks up the figure of the man.

They sold them everything from beds to roses,
    subscriptions to the beauty magazines,
Synthetic covers for their chairs and sofas
    and the first electric curlers ever seen.

Every household appliance they could dream of
    to make life easy in the modern home:
A floor waxer with two rotating brushes,
    a waffle iron that turned off on its own.

Holds the man as if balanced on the ledge of Mrs. Robson's balcony.

Prudish Mrs. Robson saw them coming
    and quickly locked her door up good and tight.
No snake of a salesman or Jehovah's witness
    tempted her to take the fatal bite.

Hangs the man by the arms over the Lepage balcony railing, as if he's on his knees to the mother.

My mother loved the salesman's demonstrations;
    he'd get down on his knees to flaunt his wares;
But he and she both knew we had no money —
    he'd not get any richer than he did upstairs.

Slides the man through the side window of the apartment
below the Lepages'. Through the living room window we see
Robert's hand pulling down a blind. Then he puts a figure of
the Great Dane out on the balcony.

But if the charmer called on our concierge,
    the blinds went down and music softly played,
And when the dog was put outside, we knew it:
    the rookie salesman was doing a roaring trade.

While her husband cursed his job down in the port,
    unloading crates from sunrise to sundown,
She cheated on him with no hint of shame,
    getting laid by the cutest boys in town.

My mother did not judge the woman's frolics,
    and to her face was perfectly polite,
But felt by turns both scandalized and jealous —
    her own husband was absent every night.

She sat outside and smoked her cigarettes,
    condemned to live a lonely purgatory:
Trapped between the Blessed Virgin Mary
    and the Woman Taken in Adultery.

As he exits backstage, Robert gives the building a shove and it
rotates 90 degrees.

SNACK BAR

A typical snack bar from the 1960s, low lighting.

A counter, three fixed-base stools with swivel seats, and a magnetic menu board with movable letters. Above it is a sign saying "Noctiluc," the name of the snack bar. On the board are the words:

UTOPIE

SÉPARATISTE

CANICHE EN RUT

DU MAGHREB

ESPRIT

EPISCOPAL

BRISÉ

HF*

Robert enters the snack bar with a flashlight, shining it around. On the counter we see a ketchup bottle, mustard, vinegar,

---

* SEPARATIST DREAMS / EPISCOPAL HE-DOG IN FUR BRA / GHOST POET.

paper napkins, etc. He runs his finger across a thick layer of dust on the first stool and spins the second one. He finds a dirty needle on floor and puts it on the menu board ledge, then looks at the board curiously. He puts his flashlight on the floor so it lights up the board, and rearranges the letters so they spell:

POUTINE

PATATES FRITES

CHIEN CHAUD

HAMBURGER

SPRITE

PEPSI COLA

BIERES*

He picks up the flashlight and goes behind the counter. He points the flashlight at the shelves and they light up.

Slow, distorted music can be heard in the distance.

He lifts a cover off some fresh-looking pastries. He touches a clock on the back wall and its face lights up. He looks in the salt and flour tins. He shines the flashlight on a beverage dispenser, which lights up, showing the circulating orange drink, then on a neon sign in the window saying "24 H", which flickers and then comes on. He takes a bottle of pop from under the counter, opens it, takes a swig and puts it down. He picks up a cap like the one his father wore in the taxi-driver photo. He dusts it off and puts it on, then sits down on a stool with his back to the audience.

---

* HAMBURGER AND FRIES / HOTDOGS / POUTINE / SPRITE / FANTA / PEPSI-COLA / BEER.

Music transitions into old-time big band, laid-back but louder.

Under the clock on the wall facing him, we can now see the kitchen through the serving hatch and the cook, visible only from thigh to shoulder, going about his business.

Robert's father lights a cigarette, looks at a newspaper, eats a hamburger, drinks from the pop bottle.

He stretches to rouse himself. He puts on his glasses to look at the bill, dumps the coins from his pocket onto the counter, picks out the exact change, then adds a tip. He looks pointedly at what little is left before putting it back in his pocket. He looks at his watch and leans over to say goodbye to the cook through the serving hatch, but he's busy. He shrugs and gets up to leave.

On the way out he goes to the menu board and replaces the "P" in POUTINE *with an "R".*

As he exits, the snack bar rotates and the big band piece ends.

TAXI AT NIGHT NO. 2

*The building rotates and stops at an angle, with the left wall
and the front facing the audience.*

*Night lighting, with only the Lepage balcony and the Saint
Moore living room window lit up.*

*Robert enters stage right and stops, creating a giant shadow on
the wall.*

*A figure of Robert as a child lies on top of a sleeping bag on the
balcony. Louis appears in the Saint Moore window and sits
down at the piano.*

> On hot summer nights I camp out on the balcony,
>   snuggled in my sleeping bag alone.
> Here I'm free to think my thoughts in peace,
>   but my fidgety feet have ideas of their own.
>
> Is that a UFO in the starless sky,
>   or is that Saturn, fooling me again?

Downstairs Louis Saint Moore is sleepless too;
    he sits down at the piano and starts playing.

Chopin's Nocturne in C Minor, Op. 48, No. 1 plays softly.

Unlike pop, classical has the power
    to awaken inner worlds we barely know
Though I'm still young, I feel a deep nostalgia
    for things I must have lived lifetimes ago.

*The taxi enters stage right, headlights on, and stops in front of
887. Robert props the figure of himself as a child against the
balcony railing.*

Then suddenly I hear his taxi coming,
    and blinded by the dazzle of its lights
I jump to my feet, delirious with hope;
    perhaps he's finished working for the night.

He parks his car and lights a cigarette,
    takes out his notepad, checks his chits are signed,
While Louis Saint Moore plays with all his heart,
    and Chopin weaves a spell around my mind.

A taxi driver's brain can hold its own
    against a piano player's any day.
A pianist has to know where all the notes are,
    and how to find them quickly as he plays.

Likewise, my father's spatial memory
    is a trusted map that he can leave in charge;

As the city swells, so does his hippocampus
  to the point of being abnormally enlarged.

He may well know the name of every parkway,
  of every street and lane and avenue,
But as to what his children do all evening,
  he doesn't have a single blessed clue.

In this waking dream of a summer night,
  will my hero turn and see me yet?
I wave to him as I lean against the railing
  of an apartment that has buried him in debt.

A muffled dispatch message is heard from the taxi radio.

The dispatch calls him for another fare,
  I want to say "I miss you, can't you stay?"
But as Chopin fills me with exquisite sadness,
  he turns the key and slowly drives away.

*The taxi slowly exits stage left while Robert watches. He slips
the figure into the sleeping bag and switches off the balcony
light. Louis Saint Moore plays on, reaching the climax of the
piece as Robert exits stage right in the bluish light, his shadow
growing as he leaves, while the building rotates left and stops as
the Nocturne ends.*

THE BRAIN

*Line drawing of a cross section of the brain from above,
showing the two hemispheres, projected on the screen/wall.*

*Robert enters, wearing a jacket with a handkerchief in the
breast pocket, and stands near the screen.*

Two days left before the poetry recital, and I still
haven't managed to learn a single line of the damn
poem. My brain feels like a boxing glove and I'm
starting to get serious headaches. I'm worried, so I
phone a friend who's a neurologist and tell him what's
going on. He tries to reassure me by telling me that my
head probably already knows the whole thing, so now
I just have to learn it by *heart*.

So I go "What the hell are you talking about?"

Then he explains that the left hemisphere of our brain
is responsible for everything logical in our lives, all

that's rational, reasonable, mathematical. And that the right side is responsible for everything intuitive, emotional, creative, visionary. It sounds as if our right hemisphere is actually much more left-leaning than our left hemisphere. Then he suggests I look for a rebellious element in the poem, and that'll force my intellectual side to wake up my emotional side.

I know that sounds like a load of psychobabble, so let's compare the two hemispheres to two adjacent apartments in a building, as seen from above.

The line drawing smoothly metamorphoses into a floorplan of the Lepage and Nolet apartments on the second floor, showing furniture and occupants. The people appear as little animated blobs who race around following Robert's description.

The apartment on the left is where the Lepage family lives, a place full of intuition, emotion, and ambition, with an added element of unpredictability, namely the grandmother.

The right-hand apartment is where the Nolets live. Here's Mr. Nolet pacing up and down. He's an accountant — a logical, rational, mathematically minded man.

Enter the rebellious element, Nancy Nolet, who arrives home drunk in the early hours of the morning as usual. She'd be far happier in the Lepage world, but she's a prisoner in the Nolet hemisphere.

Her husband is waiting up to give her hell. They start arguing and screaming at each other so loudly that one of the kids wakes up in fright and starts to cry, which wakes another kid, a third, a fourth, and so on. When all the children are wide awake, they decide to run and hide in the kitchen. But as no domestic scene is complete without witnesses, the parents go to the kitchen too. They make such a racket that it wakes up the Lepage hemisphere. My father gathers everyone in the living room, to my brother Dave's annoyance. The Nolet children decide to come and hide out at our place. Their parents continue to scream, slam doors, throw knick-knacks and plates at each other. My father decides to call the police. The police arrive, knock on the door. Mr. Nolet answers. The police enter, separate them. They try to mediate. Mr. Nolet strikes them as perfectly rational, and Mrs. Nolet as completely hysterical. They decide to take Nancy back to the police station for the night. Mr. Nolet, a little sheepish, comes over to collect his children. He orders them back to bed, each to their own bedroom, as if nothing has happened.

Screen fades to black.

The next morning, Nancy Nolet comes back from the police station and demands a divorce for the second time. Her husband refuses. They agree to continue living in the same apartment, for the time being, trapped in their two solitudes.

FLAGS

Robert moves to upstage centre, takes out a small flag from his pocket, unfolds it and holds it in front of him.

Before 1965, the Canadian flag looked like this. It was called the Red Ensign. Very few francophones in Quebec identified with this flag, mostly because it was red, a colour usually associated with the English, and because the little British flag in the corner here was a constant reminder that they had been conquered and would always have to live under the British Crown.

Lester B. Pearson, the Liberal Prime Minister of Canada at the time, is worried about the rise of separatism in Quebec, and he decides to change the Canadian flag to try to bring the Québécois back into the fold. So he appoints a flag committee and asks them to make a proposal.

He shows the back of the flag.

And this is the little marvel they came up with. People called it "Pearson's Pennant."

In the middle, the three maple leaves quite fairly represent Canada's cultural makeup at that time: the francophones, the anglophones, and the First Nations. The blue stripes on each side are a reminder that Canada is a vast country stretching from the Pacific Ocean to the Atlantic Ocean. But the beauty of this proposal is that it contains the colours of the flags of both France and Great Britain, the two founding nations of Canada.

John Diefenbaker, leader of the Conservative opposition, doesn't think there's enough red on the flag and calls for a national referendum on the question. But Lester B. Pearson, who is head of a minority government, doesn't want to lose power over a flag. So he asks the committee to come up with a compromise.

With a shake, it turns into the current Canadian maple leaf flag.

And ever since, francophones, anglophones and First Nations have lived under a single flag bearing the colours of the English majority.

PARC DES BRAVES NO. 2

Video shot of Parc des Braves as seen earlier. Model of park entrance slides in with numerous figurines crowded on the sidewalk. Robert attaches the flag to a flagpole on the right of the Monument des Braves.

Charles de Gaulle is visiting Quebec
    to renew the ties of friendship, and to show
That France is now disposed to make amends
    for ditching us two hundred years ago.

My father wakes us at the crack of dawn
    so we can find a spot where the view is grand;
And when the parade comes marching down the street,
    we'll have our places right where the big shots stand.

On the asphalt, between the pressing crowds,
    are painted lilies, the Quebec fleur-de-lys.
The General in his Lincoln runs them over,
    as majestic as a fox among the geese.

The people cheer and wave their flags and cry;
   the great procession slows down to a crawl.
As the president drives past, the shout goes up:
   "Long Live la France!" and "Long Live Charles de
   Gaulle!"

*Robert puts a figure of de Gaulle standing in a model
convertible Lincoln on the road in front of the crowd. He sets
his cellphone in the car. As he pushes the car along, the passing
crowd is projected onto the screen behind as filmed from his
phone, and "La Marseillaise" plays.*

We waited hours for such a fleeting glimpse,
   yet brief as it was, nothing ever erases
My vivid memory of the crowd that day:
   The nation's hopes were written on their faces.

*As Robert reverses the car slowly back again, the faces of the
jubilant crowd pass slowly by on the screen and "La
Marseillaise" plays in reverse.*

*He pushes the car quickly ahead again: the image is blurred
and "La Marseillaise" plays in fast forward.*

*Robert exits stage right while the model exits stage left, and the
blurry video continues of the passing landscape from Quebec
to Montreal, as if thousands of people were lining the route all
the way.*

"La Marseillaise" ends.

Video dissolves to close-up of Robert's breast pocket.

He folds back the handkerchief to reveal a figure of de Gaulle, as if standing on the balcony of Montreal City Hall giving his historic speech. De Gaulle jumps up and down frantically in his pocket as the soundtrack plays.

Voice of Charles de Gaulle: "La France entière sait, voït, entend, ce qui se passe ici et je puis vous dire qu'elle en vaudra mieux! Vive Montréal! Vive le Québec! Vive le Québec libre! Vive le Canada français et vive la France!"

Dissolve back to shot of Parc des Braves, this time at night. Stars and spectacular fireworks fill the sky. Robert moves closer to the screen.

The terrace at the Parc des Braves that night
    is lit up by a huge fireworks display.
Showers of sparks rain down on the crowd below;
    the roar of explosives takes your breath away.

The General's message couldn't be any clearer;
    most people in Quebec are over the moon—
But for my father, tired and disappointed,
    his hero's speech is like a lead balloon.

"This great man, who liberated France,"
    my father says, as the fireworks shoot up higher,
"Should have known enough to hold his tongue
    instead of pouring oil on the fire."

CLOCK

The fireworks gradually morph into neurons and dendrites.
Synapses fire off here and there. Sound of crackling electric
arcs.

Luminous transmitters carry signals
    across the gap where neurons intersect.
These moving bright transmitters run our brains,
    unless the neurons start to disconnect.

With Alzheimer's, the neurons cease to fire;
    at first the hippocampus is destroyed,
Slowly the brain transforms into Swiss cheese,
    and tangled toxic proteins fill the void.

Some of the neurons darken. Shadowy patches appear. Visual
effect of hurtling through brain cells as if through space.

My grandmother is lost in time and space;
    her moods will flip without us knowing why.

Her laughter turns to tears and then to rage —
we have to act, our options have run dry.

A clock face is clumsily drawn on the screen.

The doctor does the stock examination:
  do you know your last name? and your first?
Now please draw a picture of a clock face
  with all the numbers correctly interspersed.

A second, third, then fourth clock face are drawn, each less
accurate than the last.

My poor father is absolutely stunned
  when he realizes she is so far gone;
It makes him sad to see her clocks are like
  something his youngest children might have drawn.

"Most of her faculties are breaking down;
  she can barely speak, you say she tends to roam.
It's clear to me she's lost her memory,
  perhaps it's time to put her in a home."

BUNK BED

The last clock disappears from the screen. We see the silhouette of a bunk bed through the backlit screen. Robert slides the screen away right, takes a flashlight from the top bunk and shines it on the lower bunk, where a child is asleep. He sits on the bed and gently strokes her shoulder and long hair. Putting the flashlight down, he takes off her red blanket and hangs it from the top bunk on one side, then takes another red blanket from the top bunk and hangs it on the other side. He pins them up like opera drapes to the bed posts and addresses the audience.

This is where theatre all began, for me: in a bunk bed with my sister Lynda in a children's bedroom in Apartment 5, 887 Murray Avenue, in the Montcalm district of Quebec city.

But the true origins of theatre go back much further, to time immemorial.

He uses a white sheet from the top bunk to create a translucent screen over the lower bunk. He climbs in behind it and kneels at the foot of the bed.

To a night when a group of men and women gathered in some quarry around a fire to keep warm, and to tell stories.

With the flashlight on the bed as the light source, he appears in shadow play, warming his hands over a fire. He illustrates the rest of his account by making shadow animals with his hands.

Then suddenly one of them had the idea of using his shadow to illustrate his story. With the light from the fire, he made larger-than-life creatures appear on the walls of the quarry. The others, astounded, recognized in his shadow figures the strong and the weak, the oppressed and the oppressor, mortals and the gods.

And so you can see in the simplest shadow play of a child the very origins of theatre.

Robert's younger sister Lynda wakes up. She sits up opposite him and yawns. Robert gives her a little poke; she dodges it and pulls his hair. Then she makes a flying bird with hand shadows. Incredulous, Robert sticks his head around the curtain to watch her shadow play. He withdraws his head and motions her to come closer, strokes her hair. She shoves him away and they start a hand-clap game which quickly degenerates into a pillow fight. Feathers fly out of the pillows, the sheet shakes violently and then comes down, revealing Robert alone on the bed. He takes off his shirt, is now wearing a black T-shirt and pants. As he moves upstage, the bedroom disappears.

CONSERVATOIRE

Stage in darkness except for light on Robert.

I recently went back to the Conservatoire d'art dramatique de Québec, where I studied theatre thirty-odd years ago, to watch a production by students in their final year. They were doing *The Birds* by Aristophanes. Unfortunately I'd been told the wrong time and arrived forty-five minutes late.

Mimes conversation as he speaks.

What I did manage to see completely blew me away. It was Aristophanes' genius, of course, but mostly it was the masterful performances by the actors. I was so moved that instead of escaping right after the show, as I usually do, I stayed for the little opening-night celebration to have a drink and talk with the students.

At some point in the evening, the director of the

Conservatoire joined me at the bar.

I congratulated him and told him how impressed I was that today's students had such a command of the language. In my day we were incapable of reciting the great classical texts. It was the heyday of political theatre, so I guess the teachers felt they had to give us techniques for getting our message across in noisy places like factories, parks, and public spaces. The theatre they taught was much more physical, like mime, mask, commedia dell'arte, clowning. Clearly times have changed, I said, and there's more emphasis now on diction, voice technique, phrasing — because that's what brings in the bucks!

The director of the Conservatoire replied, "You know what, the curriculum hasn't changed that much over the years. The students have better diction now because they come from a higher social class than before. Now you have to pay to go to the Conservatoire, not like in your day when it was all free. Nowadays hardly anyone who comes for an audition is from a working-class or rural background. They couldn't afford it anyway."

He says it to my face, just like that!

He claps his hands and the lighting changes.

PETIT SÉMINAIRE

That reminded me of when I was in seventh grade and I decided to take up my Uncle Maurice's challenge and sit the entrance exams for Quebec city's prestigious private schools.

The Petit Séminaire and the Collège des Jésuites held their entrance exams jointly during Easter. I went with my best friend at the time, Charles, the son of a well-known Quebec city judge. For two long days, we answered every question in the most exhaustive tests on every subject. I remember doing very well and feeling very proud of myself. Of course, we had to wait a few weeks to get the answer. Then one morning at school, we were handed a little envelope with a beige card in it. On one side was printed:

EXCELLENT
VERY GOOD
GOOD

AVERAGE

POOR

VERY POOR

And on the other side:

ACCEPTED

REFUSED

On my friend Charles's card, the boxes "Average" and
"Accepted" had been checked. On mine, "Excellent"
was checked, but I'd been refused.

I was confused. I thought for sure they'd made a
mistake.

*The light increases slowly on the rotating building, which stops
with the rear wall facing the audience. Night lighting. The
figures of Robert and his mother are visible in the back room of
the Lepage apartment.*

That night I went home and begged my mother to get
in touch with someone at the Petit Séminaire or the
Collège des Jésuites to find out what had happened.
She managed to get hold of a friendly priest, who
agreed to have another look at my file. He tells her,
"Indeed, by the looks of things your son would have
been a perfect candidate for our school. But
unfortunately, I see here that his father is a taxi
driver." My mother says, "One minute, Father. Are you
saying my son can't go to your school because of his

father's social status?" The priest says, "No madam, social status has nothing to do with it. It's just that we have no guarantee you'll be able to pay the tuition fees over the next five years." Lost for words, my mother hangs up. She turns to me and says, "If you say anything about this to your father, it'll destroy him."

COLD CUT

Robert opens the two panels of the rear wall to reveal his present-day kitchen again. He takes a white shirt from the closet and puts it on. The doorbell rings. Robert exits stage right, but can still be heard.

Hello?

. . .

Yes, that's me, why?

. . .

Do I have to sign something?

. . .

Okay, thanks.

He enters with an envelope. He opens it and takes out a USB flash drive and a note, which he reads:

"I managed to make a copy of your cold cut. It was quite a feat. You understand I'm counting on you to be discreet. As this could put my job in serious jeopardy, and given my disastrous financial situation, I would appreciate if you could pay me the sum of $500 for my services. Add to that $17.95 for the flash drive and $8.66 for the FedEx delivery, for a total of $526.71. A paid debt is a friend kept, as they say. Fred."

He steps into the kitchen as it rotates 90 degrees to show a side view. He takes a beer from the fridge, hesitates, then puts on headphones, opens his computer, and inserts the flash drive.

The lights go down in the kitchen so his face is lit only by the computer screen. His astonishment, disbelief, and then displeasure are evident. He snaps the computer shut and takes off the headphones. The lights go up again. He throws the envelope in the garbage, and while the kitchen rotates back he steps out into the vestibule.

He gets his cellphone from his jacket in the closet and dials a number. Sound of two rings then Fred's voicemail message.

Oh great! Hide behind your answering machine! You little chickenshit.

In a detached, cold voice, increasingly irritated and then angry.

Hello Fred, it's Robert here. I know there's not enough space on your answering machine to leave a long message, but still, it's probably quite a bit more time than you spent summing up my entire career. So let me ask you this: Does thirty-five years in the theatre mean nothing at all? If something has never been electronically or digitally recorded, does that mean it never existed? If so, then the fundamental philosophical question is this: If a tree falls in the forest, and no one is there to record it on their goddamn iPhone, does it make a sound? Am I to understand that a five-minute cameo on a Radio-Canada comedy show is worth more than thirty-five years in the theatre business? Or was that the only clip you had in your archives?

Beep indicating end of time allotted for message.

Oh stuff your voicemail up your nose!

Looks at his watch.

Now I've missed my train for Montreal. Great!

Makes another call while he puts on his jacket.

DISPATCHER: Hello, Taxi Co-op!

ROBERT: Yes, could you send a car to 225 Boulevard Bastien please. No, hang on, it's called Boulevard Louis-XIV now, 225 Boulevard Louis-XIV.

DISPATCHER: To go where?

ROBERT: Montreal.

DISPATCHER: We'll send a car right away.

ROBERT: Thank you.

Robert puts away his telephone, takes "Speak White" from the kitchen, puts on his jacket and closes the panel, which sets off a rotation. A black sliding partition and legs close the space behind him.

SOUNDCHECK

Robert stands downstage at the Monument-National theatre in Montreal, text in hand, jacket under his arm. The logo of the "Nuit de la poésie" is projected on each side.

Testing, testing, one, two.

Testing, testing, one, two. Testing.

. . .

God, that's the third time you've changed my mic! What's the problem? Is it the mic, is it the battery, or am I the problem? Because, to be honest, my patience is starting to run out of juice too.

. . .

Sorry, but that's my voice. That's just the way I speak.

. . .

One, two, testing. Is it working now?

. . .

Okay . . .

What time do we have to be back for the reading?

. . .

So that means none of us will have time to eat! Will
there be snacks in the dressing room, at least?

. . .

I know, but "Speak White" is almost at the end of the
show. That means by midnight tonight I won't have
eaten since noon.

. . .

Yes, I have a question. That prompter's box up front,
does it work?

. . .

No, I don't need anyone to be in it, but you know,
sometimes in TV galas, they put a laptop in the

prompter's box with the text scrolling along, just for reference, in case . . .

. . .

No, no, I've learned mine by heart. That's not the problem. It's just that at midnight tonight, with the fatigue, and especially on an empty stomach, your blood sugar can drop and then you can have little blanks . . .

. . .

That's right, see you later . . . Nice job, guys . . . We're all set . . . Thanks!

Robert exits stage right.

The partition slides out stage right and the building appears, rotating until it faces the audience.

MANIFESTO READ BY GAÉTAN MONTREUIL

Night lighting. In the windows of each of the eight apartments, Radio-Canada announcer Gaétan Montreuil can be seen on all the black-and-white TVs reading a special bulletin in October 1970.

"For humanitarian reasons that are obvious from the unfolding of events over the past days, and if possible to save the life of the British trade commissioner, Mr. James Richard Cross, we are reading the whole manifesto of the Front de libération du Québec.

"'Front de libération du Québec. Manifesto.

"'The Front de libération du Québec is neither the Messiah nor a modern-day Robin Hood. It is a group of Quebec workers who are determined to use every means possible to ensure that the people of Quebec take control of their own destiny.

"'The Front de libération du Québec wants total independence for Quebecers, united in a free society and purged for good of the clique of voracious sharks, the corrupt "big bosses" and their henchmen who have made Quebec their private hunting ground for "cheap labour" and unscrupulous exploitation . . .'"

Robert enters in a dark suit and white shirt, wearing running shoes and carrying a fluorescent orange shoulder bag with "Le Soleil" on it. The manifesto continues at low volume.

In the fall of 1970 my brother Dave decides to leave home and go to New Brunswick to an English high school that one of his teachers recommended. So I inherit the noble task of delivering the papers.

One evening in October, when I come back from my paper route, I find the building suspiciously quiet. I go upstairs to our apartment and find my parents and two sisters sitting in the living room watching TV. They are listening to Gaétan Montreuil read every word of the FLQ manifesto on Radio-Canada.

The situation is surreal. At one point my father turns to me and says, "The worst thing about all this is that the bastards are right. But don't get me wrong, they're not right to be doing what they're doing."

I say, "So they're right, or they're not right?"

"That's what I'm telling you. They're right about their

reasons, but they're not right to be doing what they're doing."

"Yeah, but that makes no sense. If their reasons are right, then they're right to be doing what they're doing. Why shouldn't they do it, if they're right?"

"That's the thing, they're right but they're not right. If they were right, then they'd figure out that they shouldn't be doing what they're doing. I mean, if they weren't already doing what they're doing . . . because basically, they're right."

Then the telephone rings.

Telephone rings.

My mother goes to answer it while my father and I continue our little routine. After a few minutes, she hangs up.

She comes back into the living room with a long face and announces to my father that my grandmother, whom we had put in a home that summer, died in her sleep that afternoon.

My two sisters start to cry, my mother doesn't know how to react, and my father says nothing for two whole minutes. Then he gets up, puts on his coat and his cab driver's cap and without looking back, says "I'm off to work."

I'm standing there in the middle of the room, not
knowing if I should stay for this historic event or run
after my father, because he sure isn't going to work.
He's probably gone to take refuge in his taxi in the
garage, where no one can see him crying.

*Stage lights go down. The only light is from the front entrance
light and the glow of the eight windows, which are now nothing
but TV screens showing Gaétan Montreuil reading the
Manifesto..*

"Our struggle can only be victorious.

"An awakening people cannot be kept in misery and
contempt for long.

"Long live free Quebec!

"Long live our imprisoned political comrades!

"Long live the Quebec revolution!

"Long live the Front de libération du Québec!"

*As the TV screens go off, the building rotates and disappears
into the darkness.*

PAPERBOY

Robert enters, wearing a long, bright-yellow hooded raincoat, and slings his newspaper bag over his shoulder. Autumn leaves fall gently. A pair of black leather army boots are positioned stage right.

It's raining. Robert puts his hood up.

The front page of Le Soleil, dated Wednesday, October 14, 1970, is projected on the big screen behind him. In huge letters: "L'enlèvement de Pierre Laporte" (Kidnapping of Pierre Laporte), with a photo of a heavily armed soldier standing guard in front of the Parliament building in Ottawa.

The second kidnapping raises the stakes again;
    leaders in Ottawa feel they're under attack.
Now they have a ready-made excuse,
    and the government invokes the War Measures Act.

Projection of front page, dated Friday, October 16: "La Loi sur les mesures de guerre décrétée par Ottawa" (Ottawa invokes War Measures Act) and photos of army vans and police carrying out a search.

    Hundreds are arrested without warrants,
        their houses raided on a massive scale;
    Dissenters who speak up are quickly silenced
        and without due process taken off to jail.

Projection of front page, dated Sunday, October 18: "Le cadavre de Pierre Laporte retrouvé" (Body of Pierre Laporte found) and photo of corpse in the trunk of a car.

    One morning we see the pictures in the papers:
        the Minister of Labour, yesterday,
    Was located near a military airbase,
        found dead in the trunk of a Chevrolet.

    In Montreal the situation's dire,
        but in Quebec the army is less active
    Except at Parliament and the Rue des Braves,
        where politicians and the upper class live.

Transition to live video, a close-up backward tracking shot of Robert's feet as he walks towards the boots, dropping newspapers left and right along the way.

    This lovely street is on my paper route,
        People chain their doors, sit idle in the dark;

The road's deserted except for me and my papers —
No longer afraid to hear the guard dogs bark.

*Robert stops centre stage. The camera continues backward
tracking between the boots and stops when the boots fill the
entire frame. We see the lower part of Robert's body, the
newspapers dropped on the leaf-strewn ground, and the rain
falling.*

They've put a fence in front of Jean Lesage's,
  for two long terms the premier of Quebec.
It blocks the way so no one can get near him,
  a soldier's in the doorway, just to check.

On his helmet, he wears as a disguise,
  a sodden branch he's broken off a tree;
A withered maple leaf conceals his face,
  his camouflage is all that you can see.

"Empty your bag of papers — NOW!" he says,
  and points his gun directly at my head.
I obey without a word and pray to God
  his finger doesn't slip and shoot me dead.

Inspection done, I gather up my papers
  and wonder how rewarding is his role
Of taking such a patriotic pride
  in terrorizing kids of twelve years old.

I stand up slowly under his hostile glare
  and walk away, although I'm seeing red;

I hold my tongue, but want to yell out "Idiot!
    The bombs aren't in my bag, they're in my head!"

Exits stage left.

Blackout.

SPEAK WHITE

The stage is still dark when enthusiastic applause can be heard.

A single beam from above creates a circle of light, centre downstage, just behind the prompter's box. Robert enters stage left in a three-piece suit, white open-neck shirt and black leather shoes. He stands in the circle, his left hand in his pants pocket. The applause tapers off. A low-angle beam pointing at him creates an unnaturally large shadow on the backdrop. He stands absolutely still.

*"*NUIT *de la* POÉSIE *40ᵉ* ANNIVERSAIRE*" is projected on each side of the backdrop.*

After a moment, Robert steps out of the circle of light and moves downstage left, but his shadow stays behind, moving slightly as if it were alive and breathing. Robert addresses the audience, appealing to his shadow as if to a witness.

About a minute before going on stage, I asked myself what anyone else would in such circumstances: What the hell have I let myself in for? Why did I agree to put myself on the line yet again?

But the second I walked on stage, I had my answer.

It certainly wasn't for the immense privilege and honour of reciting this legendary poem, but rather to try to impress the crowd, who that night were all big shots from the political, arts and media scenes. There were people from the federal and provincial governments, Montreal City Hall, the Canada Council for the Arts, the Conseil des arts et des lettres du Québec; there was a former member of the FLQ who drives across the Pierre Laporte Bridge every Thursday to go and give his political science class at Université Laval. There was a journalist from *Le Devoir* whose column appears every Tuesday morning, when *Le Devoir* consists of four pages folded double to make it look like eight, and who probably has no idea that the founder of the paper, Henri Bourassa, was himself told to "Speak white!" when he tried to address the House of Commons in French in 1889. And a whole slew of one-time hippies who prided themselves on having "been there at the time"

but who all arrived late because they couldn't
find a parking spot on René-Lévesque for their
brand-new SUVs with the licence plates that say
"*Québec. Je me souviens*" (Quebec. I remember).

What is it, exactly, that I'm supposed to
remember?!

Then I thought, I don't deserve to recite these
words. Any more than the people sitting in this
room deserve to hear them. And I thought,
whatever I inherited from my father, it certainly
wasn't his great humility. And I thought, that bill
for $465 I can feel in my left pocket, which was the
cost of my taxi fare from Quebec City to Montreal
so I could get to this event, and which I paid
without even batting an eye, would have
represented more than a month's wages for my
father. And then I thought, in all truthfulness,
only someone like him would have the authority
to read these words.

He returns to the middle of the circle of light. Surtitles in
English appear as Robert recites Michèle Lalonde's
original bilingual poem.

speak white
il est si beau de vous entendre
parler de Paradise Lost
ou du profil gracieux et anonyme qui tremble dans les
   sonnets de Shakespeare

nous sommes un peuple inculte et bègue
mais ne sommes pas sourds au génie d'une langue
parlez avec l'accent de Milton et Byron et Shelley et Keats
speak white
et pardonnez-nous de n'avoir pour réponse
que les chants rauques de nos ancêtres
et le chagrin de Nelligan

speak white
parlez de choses et d'autres
parlez-nous de la Grande Charte
ou du monument à Lincoln
du charme gris de la Tamise
de l'eau rose du Potomac
parlez-nous de vos traditions
nous sommes un peuple peu brillant
mais fort capable d'apprécier
toute l'importance des crumpets
ou du Boston Tea Party

mais quand vous really speak white
quand vous get down to brass tacks
pour parler du Gracious living
et parler du standard de vie
et de la Grande société
un peu plus fort alors speak white
haussez vos voix de contremaîtres
nous sommes un peu durs d'oreille
nous vivons trop près des machines
et n'entendons que notre souffle au-dessus des outils

speak white and loud
qu'on vous entende
de Saint-Henri à Saint-Domingue
oui quelle admirable langue
pour embaucher
donner des ordres
fixer l'heure de la mort à l'ouvrage
et de la pause qui rafraîchit
et ravigote le dollar

speak white
tell us that God is a great big shot
and that we're paid to trust him
speak white
parlez-nous production profits et pourcentages
speak white
c'est une langue riche
pour acheter
mais pour se vendre
mais pour se vendre à perte d'âme
mais pour se vendre
ah!
speak white
big deal

mais pour vous dire
l'éternité d'un jour de grève
pour raconter
une vie de peuple-concierge
mais pour rentrer chez nous le soir
à l'heure où le soleil s'en vient crever au-dessus des ruelles
mais pour vous dire oui que le soleil se couche oui
chaque jour de nos vies à l'est de vos empires
rien ne vaut une langue à jurons
notre parlure pas très propre
tachée de cambouis et d'huile

speak white
soyez à l'aise dans vos mots
nous sommes un peuple rancunier
mais ne reprochons à personne
d'avoir le monopole
de la correction de langage

dans la langue douce de Shakespeare
avec l'accent de Longfellow
parlez un français pur et atrocement blanc
comme au Vietnam au Congo
parlez un allemand impeccable
une étoile jaune entre les dents
parlez russe parlez rappel à l'ordre parlez répression
speak white
c'est une langue universelle
nous sommes nés pour la comprendre
avec ses mots lacrymogènes
avec ses mots matraques

speak white
tell us again about Freedom and Democracy
nous savons que liberté est un mot noir
comme la misère est nègre
et comme le sang se mêle à la poussière des rues d'Alger
   ou de Little Rock

speak white
de Westminster à Washington relayez-vous
speak white comme à Wall Street
white comme à Watts
be civilized
et comprenez notre parler de circonstance
quand vous nous demandez poliment
how do you do
et nous entendez vous répondre
we're doing all right
we're doing fine
we
are not alone

nous savons
que nous ne sommes pas seuls

*Surtitles**

speak white / so nice it is to hear you / speak of Paradise
Lost / or of the graceful, elusive figure trembling in
Shakespeare's sonnets / we are an ignorant and
stammering people / but not deaf to the genius of a
language / so speak with the accent of Milton and Byron
and Shelley and Keats / speak white / and forgive us if we
can only reply / with the raucous songs of our ancestors /
and the sorrow of Nelligan / speak white / speak of this
and that / speak of the Magna Carta / or of the Lincoln
Memorial / of the grey charm of the Thames / or the pink

---

* Surtitles accompany the recitation of the original bilingual poem in the
English production of the play. They are not to be considered an official
translation.

waters of the Potomac / speak about your traditions / we
are not an especially brilliant people / but quite able to
appreciate / the great importance of crumpets / or the
Boston Tea Party / but when you really speak white /
when you get down to brass tacks / to speak about
Gracious Living / and speak about standards of living /
and of the Great Society / a little louder then, speak
white / raise your foremen's voices / we are a little hard of
hearing / we live too close to the machines /all we can
hear over the tools is our own breathing / speak white
and loud / so we can hear you / from Saint-Henri to
Santo-Domingo / yes such an admirable tongue / in
which to hire / give orders /establish time of dying
at work / and schedule the pause that refreshes / and
freshens up the dollar / speak white / tell us that God is a
great big shot / and that we're paid to trust him / speak
white / talk production profits and percentages / speak
white / it's a rich language / for buying / but for selling
oneself / but for selling one's soul / but for selling
oneself / ah! / speak white / big deal / but to tell you
about / the eternity of a day on strike / or recount / the
life of a janitor-people / but to come home at night / when
the sun sets over our back alleys / but for telling you yes
that the sun does set yes / every day of our lives east of
your empires / nothing can beat a language of curses /
our unclean idiom / stained with oil and axle grease /
speak white / feel at ease with your words / we're a
resentful people / but we don't begrudge anyone / for
having a monopoly / on language correction / in
Shakespeare's soft tongue / with the accent of
Longfellow / speak a pure and atrociously white French /

as in Vietnam or in Congo / speak an impeccable
German / a yellow star between your teeth / speak
Russian speak re-call to order speak repression / speak
white / it's a universal language / we were born to
understand it / with its teargas words / its billyclub words /
speak white / tell us again about Freedom and
Democracy / we know liberty is a black word / as misery
is Black / and as blood mingles with dust in the streets of
Algiers or Little Rock / speak white / from Westminster
to Washington take turns / speak white as in Wall Street /
white as in Watts / be civilized /and understand our
conventional answer / when you ask us politely / how do
you do / and hear us reply / we're doing all right / we're
doing fine / we / are not alone / we know / we are not
alone

Blackout.

TAXI IN THE GARAGE

The headlights of a car light up and shine straight at the audience. Robert in his yellow raincoat enters the garage and goes to the passenger door.

The car, evidently his father's taxicab, consists of a bench seat, the steering wheel, the taxi meter, the dispatch radio, with the headlights and the roof light on.

Robert mimes opening the door, gets in the passenger side and closes the door. Sound effects of the car door.

He takes off his hood, fiddles with the taxi meter and then turns on the radio.

We hear the Québécois version of "Bang Bang" sung by a pop star of the day. He takes a handkerchief from his pocket, unfolds it and holds it out to the empty driver's seat.

The roof light goes off and the headlights increase in intensity until for a few seconds they completely dazzle the spectators.

Return to pre-dazzle lighting.

Now Robert's father is at the wheel in his coat and taxi driver's cap, holding the handkerchief, his head bent over the wheel.

He sits up, takes off his glasses and cleans them.

He wipes his eyes, puts his glasses on, blows his nose and puts the handkerchief in his coat pocket.

Looking over to the passenger side, he points to the radio, as if asking a question.

He turns the knob and stops at a station playing the melancholy country song "Leavin' On Your Mind" by Patsy Cline.

He takes out a cigarette and offers it to his passenger. He shrugs and lights the cigarette himself.

He smokes it slowly, lost in thought.

As if shaken from his reverie by the passenger, he shows him the time on his watch and with a hand gesture indicates other places.

He starts the engine and puts the car in gear. Rotation begins.

Sound effects of engine starting up and car leaving.

The building appears, front facing the audience. Night lighting.

The model taxi drives downstage right, headlights and roof light on, and out stage left.

As the song ends, the lights in the apartments go out one by one, ending with the Lepage apartment. Then the very last light, the entrance light of 887 Murray Avenue, is turned off.

Blackout.

© Julie Perreault

ROBERT LEPAGE is a multidisciplinary artist and founder of the creative company Ex Machina. An imaginative director, playwright, actor, and film director, Lepage has been hailed by international critics for his highly original theatrical works that incorporate the use of new technologies and defy boundaries.

LOUISA BLAIR is a Quebec city writer, translator, and editor.